BALLOONS

Clive Minnitt

Introduction

Ever since the Bristol International Balloon Fiesta celebrated its inaugural weekend in September 1979, those who are fortunate to live in the Bristol area have been treated to the wonderful sight of colourful hot-air balloons flying over the city and surrounding countryside.

The first Fiesta was inspired by Don Cameron who has done so much to promote hot-air ballooning. It is the largest of its kind in Europe and, surely, one of the best free public events in the UK. Incredibly, it is attended by up to half a million people each year and this four-day event has become as much a symbol of the city as Isambard Kingdom Brunel and the Clifton Suspension Bridge, Concorde, the ss *Great Britain*, Wallace & Gromit and Banksy.

If only the Montgolfier brothers, who flew the first manned hot-air balloons in 1783, were able to witness the growth of this extremely photogenic form of air travel. We must be grateful for their pioneering endeavours.

Although Bristol is a major tour de force of ballooning in the UK, the growth of this sedate form of air travel has seen it become a worldwide phenomenon. In recent years there have been many much-publicised attempts by high-profile personalities to be the first to fly a hot-air balloon over the Atlantic, cross the Pacific, fly non-stop around the world and reach the highest possible altitude. These have caught the attention of the public and become headline news.

Of course, launches aren't restricted to the Fiesta's beautiful amphitheatre setting, neither are they seasonally dependent. Throughout the year, whenever the notoriously changeable British weather conditions are suitable the balloon crews are eager to take advantage. Stable conditions are ideal with a low wind speed; rain and volatile weather are a definite no-no! The nation's favourite topic of conversation, the weather, is never far away from a balloonist's lips!

Spotting hot-air balloons in flight is so uplifting, certainly addictive, and can also generate impromptu changes in people's behaviour. I've often witnessed workers totally distracted from their tasks whenever a balloon appears. Motorists have been known to pull over onto the hard shoulder whilst driving along the M4 and M5 motorways to stop and photograph a sky full of balloons following a successful mass ascent.

I too became smitten with ballooning and many years ago a work colleague and I almost purchased a second-hand balloon and basket. We were sufficiently keen to regularly attend the theory lessons held at Bristol Airport. At the time I was at a crossroads in my life and thought long and hard about which direction to turn. The decision to enjoy a lengthy backpacking trip instead, paradoxically helped to spark off my own interest in photography.

I'm grateful for having had the opportunity to experience hot-air ballooning first-hand and was surprised on several counts. Travelling with the wind meant that there was no sense of movement whatsoever. The ascent was serenely calm and the inevitable concerns over being so close to a several thousand foot drop were soon put to rest. It was heavenly!

On the downside, as it were, I've been a passenger in a basket which landed on a barbed-wire fence (the only man-made object present for miles in the middle of the Australian Outback); partly demolished an overgrown hedge in the Cotswolds whilst travelling backwards in a bouncing basket, and in Bristol, on the most wind-free day imaginable, once airborne flew nowhere at all.

My favourite recollection is of flying over urban areas chatting with those who leave the post-dawn cosiness of their front rooms to wave at us from their gardens below. How bizarre it must be for them to hear requests for lashings of tea and bacon butties from a merry band of low-flying strangers hovering over their rooftops!

After such exhilarating flights the only conclusion I could possibly draw is that hot-air ballooning is definitely on the up!

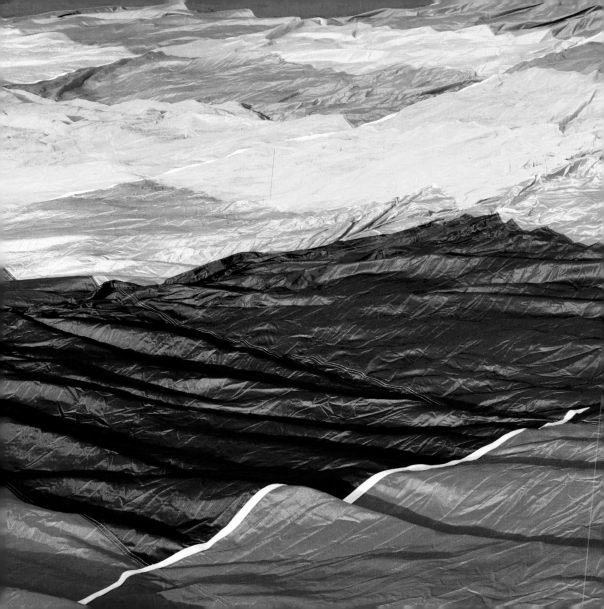

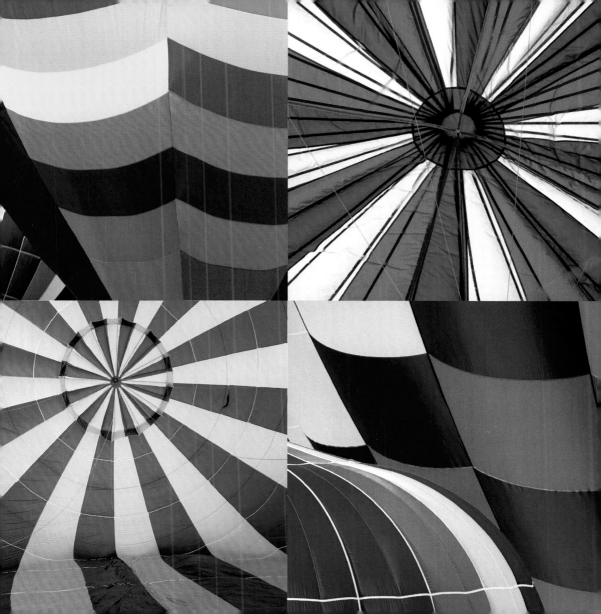

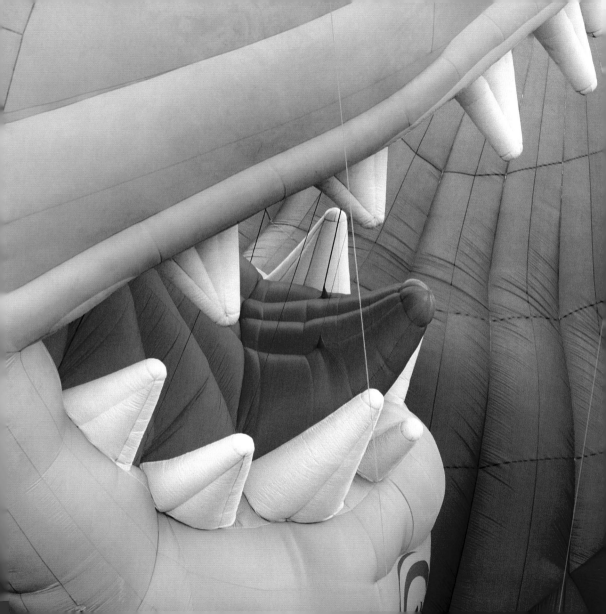

Building
Society
Bath Balloons.co.uk
for flights call
01225 466888

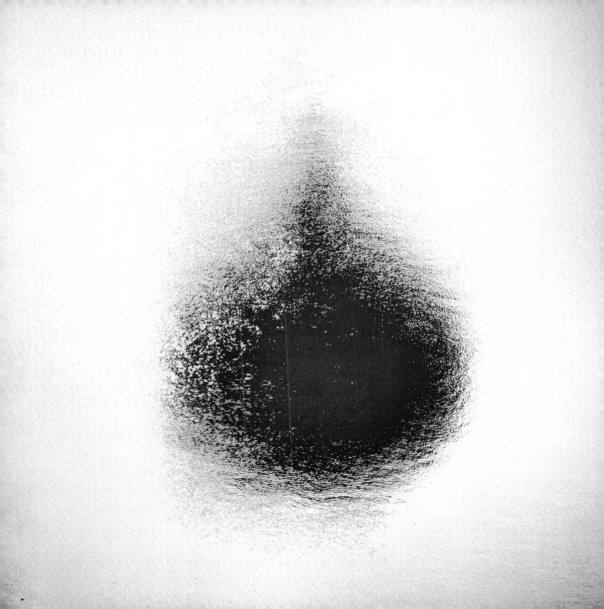

About Clive Minnitt

Clive Minnitt is a freelance photographer and writer living in Bristol, England.

Clive's latest book Bristol Hot-Air Balloons, follows in the footsteps of his successful The GORILLAS have landed, published in 2011. Details of all Clive's titles can be found on page 79.

Both Fuji and Panasonic have used his images to advertise their own products and his work has been widely exhibited at a number of galleries including Christies and the Mall Galleries in London, and Cardiff's St David's Hall.

In May 2002, Clive led his first photographic holiday for the UK-based company Light & Land for whom he has become one of the most established tour leaders. He has led over 45 tours and workshops to many locations across the UK, Europe, USA and Cuba. If you would like to join Clive on a photographic experience of a lifetime please visit www.lightandland to see which tours are presently on offer.

Many magazines and books have featured Clive's work and for several years he has been a regular contributor to Outdoor Photography magazine. He also presents his images and photographic techniques to many organisations and societies, including the National Trust.

To see more of Clive's work or purchase a copy of this book please visit
www.minnitt.co.uk

Photographic notes

During the early 1990's when my interest in photography was at a fledgling stage I joined a local camera club for a short while. I remember noticing that there were very few, if any, images of hot-air balloons entered into competitions and exhibitions.

I quickly learnt that the inclusion of such images was considered bad form; a case of familiarity breeding contempt. Subconsciously, I must have been affected as during the following years I felt little or no desire to photograph the balloons. Although they were a beautiful sight it seems that I had become no more than a casual observer.

My waning interest was halted one gorgeous evening whilst watching a swathe of hot-air balloons glide from their take-off site at Ashton Court Estate and head towards the floating harbour. From my viewpoint, standing at the edge of the Clifton Suspension Bridge, I witnessed a breathtaking sight especially as the balloons were accompanied by a particularly atmospheric cloud formation.

Since that moment in 2008, the balloons have grabbed my attention and any sighting of them spurred me into action. It became obvious that on my doorstep there was an excellent photographic challenge and an exciting subject for a potential new book.

I had to think laterally in order to produce a variety of interesting images. Continually photographing balloons against a cloudless blue sky would only result in a bland body of work. Unsurprisingly, the weather forecast was my starting point. Wind speed and direction play a vital part in ballooning and it was often touch and go as to whether I would have anything to photograph.

Although the Balloon Fiesta at Ashton Court was the source of the majority of the images in this book, particularly the mass ascents, special shapes and spectators, many were made as a result of 'stalking' the balloons as they flew above Bristol. I was often able to anticipate their movement and be in position to use sections of a few well-known local landmarks to provide foreground interest.

The majority of the images were made during 2011 & 2012. Most were

Thanks to...

captured using Panasonic Lumix cameras. Primarily, I used a GF1 body with a series of interchangeable lenses from wide angle to telephoto. This was augmented with the compact model LX5. A few earlier images were captured using a Canon EOS5D mk1 and Canon 100-400mm 'L' series lens.

Whilst much of my photography involves the use of a tripod the images in this book were almost all produced with the camera handheld. Speed of thought, anticipation and the necessity to adapt to rapidly changing scenes were all vital. A tripod would have hindered rather than aided my progress.

The digital files were pre-processed either in Panasonic's SILKYPIX Developer software (to convert the RAW files) and the Canon equivalent, Digital Photo professional. Minimal post-processing work was carried out in Adobe Photoshop before converting the files to a format suitable for printing in this book.

I would like to give my sincere thanks to:

My father, Denis, for his continual encouragement and support. At the splendid age of 86 he is looking forward to his first hot-air balloon flight.

Eddie Ephraums, for his excellent design skills and invaluable input.

Phil Malpas, for his inspiration and continual prompting.

John Ellin, for keeping my IT head above water.

Sally Packer, for her PR & marketing expertise.

Martin Bates, for his proofreading skills.

Everyone involved in organising, sponsoring, piloting, crewing and participating at the annual International Hot-Air Balloon Fiesta in Bristol.

Special thanks to Don Cameron for his exceptional work and being the driving force and inspiration behind hot-air ballooning not just in Bristol but much further afield.

Clive & Jo Bailey and all at Bailey Balloons, for an exhilarating flight at the International Balloon Fiesta at Ashton Court, Bristol.

Further books by the author

In the same series of books based in Bristol, Clive Minnitt has also published:

The GORILLAS have landed

Published 2011 (ISBN 978-0-9570620-0-9)
A light-hearted look at the 61 gorillas, which invaded the Bristol city area and the minds of its inhabitants during the summer of 2011. Available at www.minnitt.co.uk
"Inspiring & brilliant photography! Clive has put a fresh spin on photographing inanimate objects." Mark Carwardine, photographer and TV & radio presenter.

Further titles:

Isle of Sark

Published in 2011 jointly with Phil Malpas. Isle of Sark documents their photographic visit to the beautiful Channel Island and is available either at www.minnitt.co.uk or www.blurb.com.
"Thank you for your beautiful book, Isle of Sark. It is an inspiration, not only to me but to my daughters and my son-in-law."
Faye Blenkhorne, Nova Scotia, Canada

Finding the Picture – A location photography masterclass

Published 2009. ISBN: 978-1902538587.
The book is aimed at every photographer who needs a helping hand at identifying suitable subject matter to photograph. The book is jointly written and photographed by Clive and his good friend and fellow Light & Land tour leader, Phil Malpas. It is lavishly illustrated with fine-art colour photography.
Limited Edition hardback version available at www.minnitt.co.uk or softback from www.amazon.co.uk.
"A must have for anyone wanting to get deeper into the art of outdoor photography. Stunning images and insightful text reveal the mental process behind how to find and take great photos." Steve Watkins, Editor's Choice, Outdoor Photography magazine

Clevedon Pier – A celebration of England's Finest Pier

Published in 2008. ISBN: 978-0954101138
The book is a collection of fine-art images, memories and anecdotes combining atmospheric contemporary photographs with a fascinating documentary of Clevedon Pier, its history and immediate environs.
Hardback available at www.minnitt.co.uk
"What a lovely book. It was an honour to be involved - even in such a minor way."
Griff Rhys Jones, comedian, writer, actor & TV presenter.

First published in Great Britain 2012
by Clive Minnitt Books
15 Longfield Road, Bishopston, Bristol BS7 9AG

A catalogue record for this book is available
from the British Library.

ISBN 978-0-9570620-1-6
Design and production by Eddie Ephraums,
Envisage Books

Printed by Advantage Digital Print